Written by Robyn Hamilton
Edited by Linda Milliken
Assistant Editor Deneen Celecia
Design by Wendy Loreen
Cover and Text Illustration by Barb Lorseyedi

About the Author

Robyn Hamilton earned her elementary teaching credential at the University of Southern California and has taught school for thirteen years. Her keen interest in ancient civilizations has been shared with her students who delve into the past with great enthusiasm.

© 1990 **EDUPRESS** • P.O. Box 883 • Dana Point, CA 92629

ISBN 1-56472-025-X

TABLE OF CONTENTS

PAGE	ACTIVITY	DESCRIPTION
3	User Guide/Literature List	*Resource*
4-5	Hieroglyphics	*Writing activity*
6	Rosetta Stone	*Clay craft*
7	Painting Style	*Paper chain*
8-9	Nile Barge	*Paper craft*
10-11	Nile Crocodiles	*Paper craft*
12	Nile Mural	*Painting—cooperative*
13	Papyrus	*Science/project*
14	Scribes	*Writing activity*
15	Measurement	*Activity*
16-17	Number Bow	*Game/cooperative*
18	Paddle Doll	*Cardboard craft*
19	Recreation	*Playground activities*
20	Wigs	*Paper craft*
21	Makeup	*Apply makeup*
22	Collar Necklace	*Straw craft/jewelry*
23	Clothing	*Costume*
24-25	Village Crafts	*Crafts*
26	Marketplace Bartering	*Cooperative activity*
27	Garden	*Planting project*
28-31	House Diorama (instructions)	*Cooperative project*
	Silos, Farmland	
	Stables, Lotus Pools	
	Reception Hall, Bedroom	
32	Feast	*Cooperative feast*
33	Bread	*Cooking*
34-35	King Tut Mask	*Cardboard craft*
36	Crook	*Craft*
37	Flail	*Craft*
38-39	Pyramids	*Paper cut out*
40	Tombs: interior mazes	*Design*
41	Temple of Amon-Re	*Painting/cooperative*
42	Mummification	*Papier-maché craft*
43	Sarcophagus	*Paper craft*
44	Scarab	*Bread dough craft*
45	Sphinx	*Drawing/cooperative*
46-48	Crowns	*Paper craft*

LITERATURE LIST

• *The Egyptian Cinderella*
by Shirley Climo;
Thomas Y. Crowell 1989.
29 pages

• *Into the Mummy's Tomb, The Real Life*
  Discovery of Tutankhamun's Treasures
by Nicholas Reeves;
Scholastic, Inc. 1992.
64 pages

• *Ancient Egypt*
by George Hart;
Alfred A. Knopf 1990.
80 pages

• *Pyramid*
by David Macaulay;
Houghton Mifflin Co. 1975.
80 pages

• *The Egyptians Pop-up*
by Anne Wild;
Tarquin Publications 1985.
30 pages

• *Hieroglyphs from A to Z*
by Peter Der Manuelian;
Museum of Fine Arts 1991.
48 pages

• *The Winged Cat, A Tale of Ancient Egypt*
by Deborah Nourse Lattimore;
HarperCollins 1992.
32 pages

• *Mummies Made in Egypt*
by Aliki;
HarperCollins 1979.
32 pages

• *What Do We Know About the Egyptians?*
by JoAnna Defrates
Simon and Schuster 1991.
45 pages

• *The Everyday Life of an Egyptian Craftsman*
by Giovanni Caselli;
P. Bedrick 1991.
32 pages

• *The Children of Egypt*
by Reijo Harkonen;
Carolrhoda Books 1991.
40 pages

• *The Land of the Pharaohs*
by Marinella Terzi;
Childrens 1992.
36 pages

• *On the Banks of the Pharaoh's Nile*
by Corinne Courtalon;
Young Discovery Library 1988.
38 pages

• *The Egypt Game*
by Zilpha Keatley Snyder;
Dell Yearling 1986.
215 pages

• *The Ancient Egyptians: Life in the Nile Valley*
by Viviane Koening;
Millbrook Press 1992.
64 pages

• *The Land of the Pharaohs*
by Marinella Terzi;
Childrens 1992.
36 pages

• *Mummy*
by James Putnam;
Alfred Knopf, Inc. 1993.
64 pages

• *Ancient Egypt*
by Daniel Cohen;
Doubleday 1990.
48 pages

HIEROGLYPHICS

HISTORICAL AID

Hieroglyphics is a form of writing in which picture symbols represent ideas and sounds. The Ancient Egyptians used hieroglyphic writing for more than 3000 years. This script is made of 750 signs, which include pictures of people, animals, plants and objects. Hieroglyphics can be written left to right, right to left or top to bottom. The clue is to start from the end the figures are facing. This method of writing was deliberately kept complicated so few could master it and only scribes were able to write it. Hieroglyphics were used on state monuments, temples, tombs and religious papyri.

PROJECT

Write a hieroglyphic message to use in a translation activity.

MATERIALS

• Writing paper

• Crayons or colored marking pens

• Tape

DIRECTIONS

1. Reproduce several copies of the hieroglyphics on the facing page for students to refer to.

2. Lead the class in writing easy words in hieroglyphics like cat, dog, goose and crocodile.

3. Have students write a message using a combination of hieroglyphics and English. Tape the messages to the wall.

4. Let students pretend to be archeologists discovering the messages.

5. Assign the translation of each hieroglyphic message to a different student.

6. Share the translations.

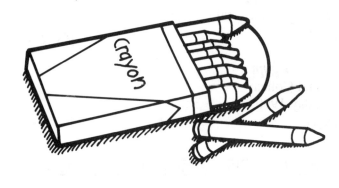

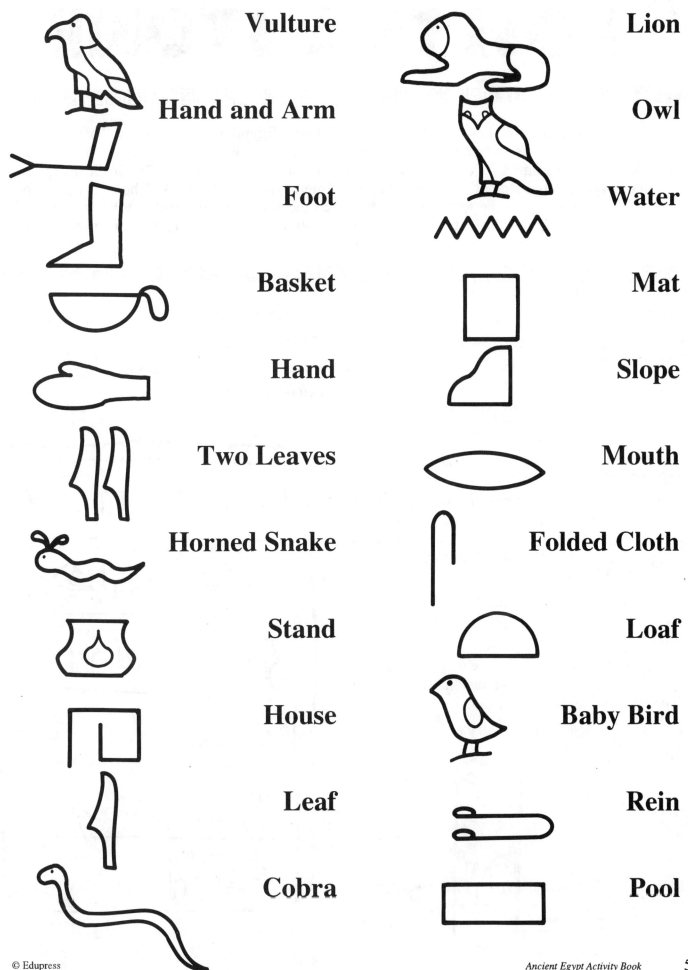

Vulture	Lion
Hand and Arm	Owl
Foot	Water
Basket	Mat
Hand	Slope
Two Leaves	Mouth
Horned Snake	Folded Cloth
Stand	Loaf
House	Baby Bird
Leaf	Rein
Cobra	Pool

ROSETTA STONE

HISTORICAL AID

The Rosetta Stone has been the key to unlocking Egyptian hieroglyphics. This piece of black basalt was discovered in 1799 A.D. near a town called Rosetta. It measures 45 inches by 28 inches (114 cm X 72 cm). The inscriptions on the stone are written in Greek, Egyptian hieroglyphics and Demotic, a simpler form of hieroglyphics. A French scholar named Jean Champollion studied the text. First he translated the Greek inscription; then he was able to learn the meaning of the Egyptian hieroglyphic characters by matching the same names from the Greek text.

PROJECT

Mold and inscribe an accurate-scale replica of the Rosetta Stone.

MATERIALS

- Clay
- Sharp pencils or toothpicks
- Black spray paint

DIRECTIONS

1. First determine an accurate-size reduction for a smaller scale Rosetta Stone. For example, to make a quarter-size, the measurement would be approximately 4-3/4 inches by 7 inches (12 cm X 18 cm).

2. Using these measurements, roll or firmly pat the clay to resemble the shape on the right. Smooth the top of the clay.

3. Refer to the hieroglyphic code on page 5 and ask students to write their own messages in the clay using a toothpick or sharp pencil.

4. Allow finished projects to dry and then spray paint black.

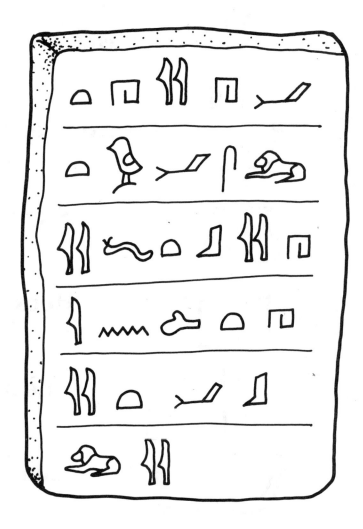

PAINTING STYLE

HISTORICAL AID

The Egyptian artists developed one of the first definite traditions in the history of the art of painting. They painted figures according to strict rules that hardly changed for thousands of years. The figures they drew looked very stiff. The head was drawn in profile while the upper body was drawn from the front and the lower body from the side. Important people in society were always drawn larger than the other people in the painting. These distinctive paintings were found on the walls of temples, palaces and tombs.

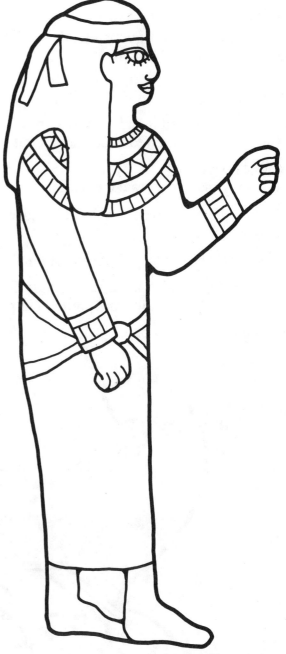

PROJECT

Make a paper chain of Egyptian figures in profile.

MATERIALS

- Pattern
- 9" by 12" (23 cm X 30 cm) Construction paper
- Colored pens
- Scissors

DIRECTIONS

1. Fold construction paper in accordion pattern lengthwise. There should be four folds.

2. Place pattern on top of the folded paper. Make sure the pattern touches both sides.

3. Cut through the pattern and four folds of paper. Do not cut where the pattern touches the edges.

4. Open and color the repeat figures. Use as a bulletin board border.

NILE BARGES

HISTORICAL AID

The Nile river and its canals provided the main means of transportation throughout Egypt. The river was a hub of activity filled with boats carrying important government officials, priests and their families on business or pleasure trips, traders transporting their goods from port to port and builders moving rock from the quarries to the many building sites. There were a variety of boats ranging from small, lightweight papyrus boats to large wooden barges with many paddles and sails. Many were manned by crews of rowers and whip-wielding overseers.

PROJECT

Make a replica of an Egyptian wooden barge to use in a diorama or Nile-river mural.

DIRECTIONS

1. Fold the tagboard in half or use a pre-folded file folder on which to trace and cut out the pattern.

2. Use crayons to decorate the barge.

3. Flatten the original fold and refold along the dotted lines. Glue the top inch of the boat halves together.

4. Complete the barge with these optional features:

   • Add a paper sail to a craft-stick mast. Secure the mast to the barge bottom by cutting a small slot, inserting the craft stick and taping it in place.

   • Add construction paper paddles or people inside the barge.

MATERIALS

• Tagboard or manila file folder
• Crayons, glue
• Pattern, following page
• Clear tape
• Craft or popsicle sticks
• Colored construction paper

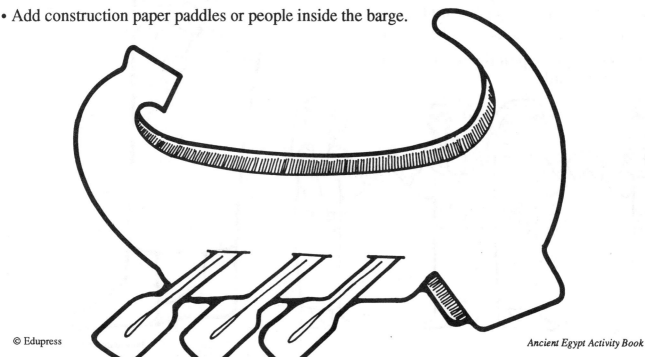

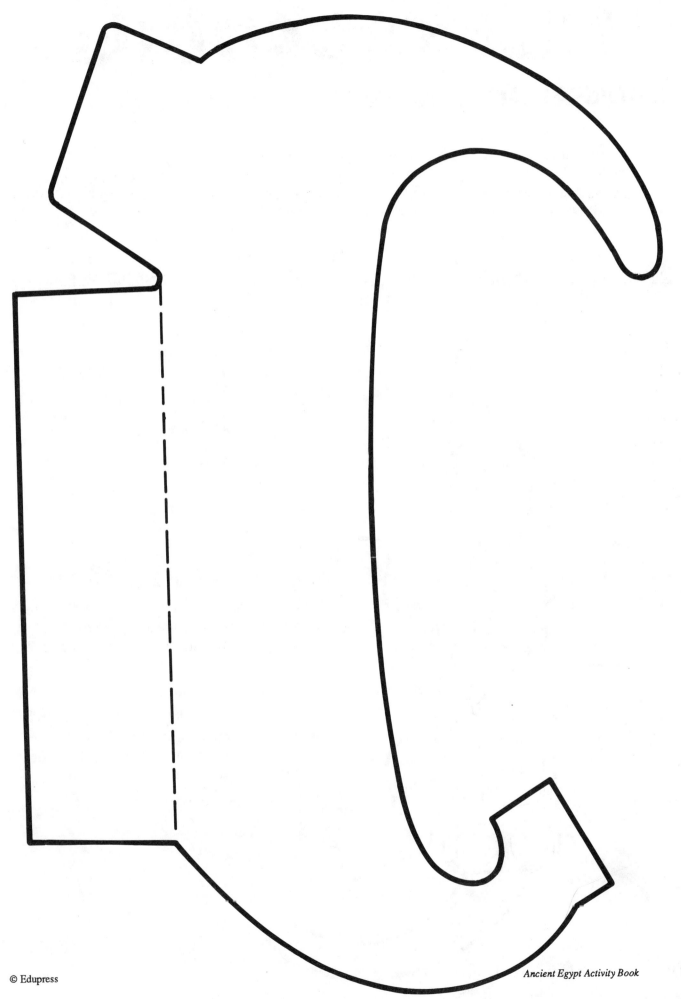

NILE CROCODILES

HISTORICAL AID

An abundance of wildlife has always thrived on the Nile. One of the most famous and feared is the Nile crocodile. In ancient Egypt, crocodiles were the symbol of the croc god, Sebek. At the city of Crocodopolis, a priest always kept a live crocodile fat and fit. When it died, it was mummified and put into a special tomb.

PROJECT

Make an egg-carton crocodile to use as a prompt for creative stories about the Nile river.

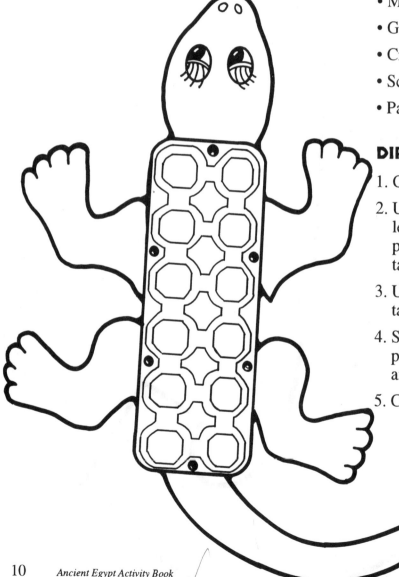

MATERIALS

- Cardboard egg carton
- Green and red construction paper
- Metal brads—six per crocodile
- Green tempera paint
- Crayons
- Scissors
- Patterns, following page

DIRECTIONS

1. Cut off the egg carton lid.

2. Use the patterns to trace and cut four green legs and two green heads. Use the head pattern to cut one red tongue. Cut one green tail.

3. Use the metal brads to attach the legs and tail to the sides and end of the egg carton.

4. Sandwich the tongue between the head pieces. Use a metal brad to attach the head and tail to each end of the crocodile.

5. Color eyes and nostrils on the head.

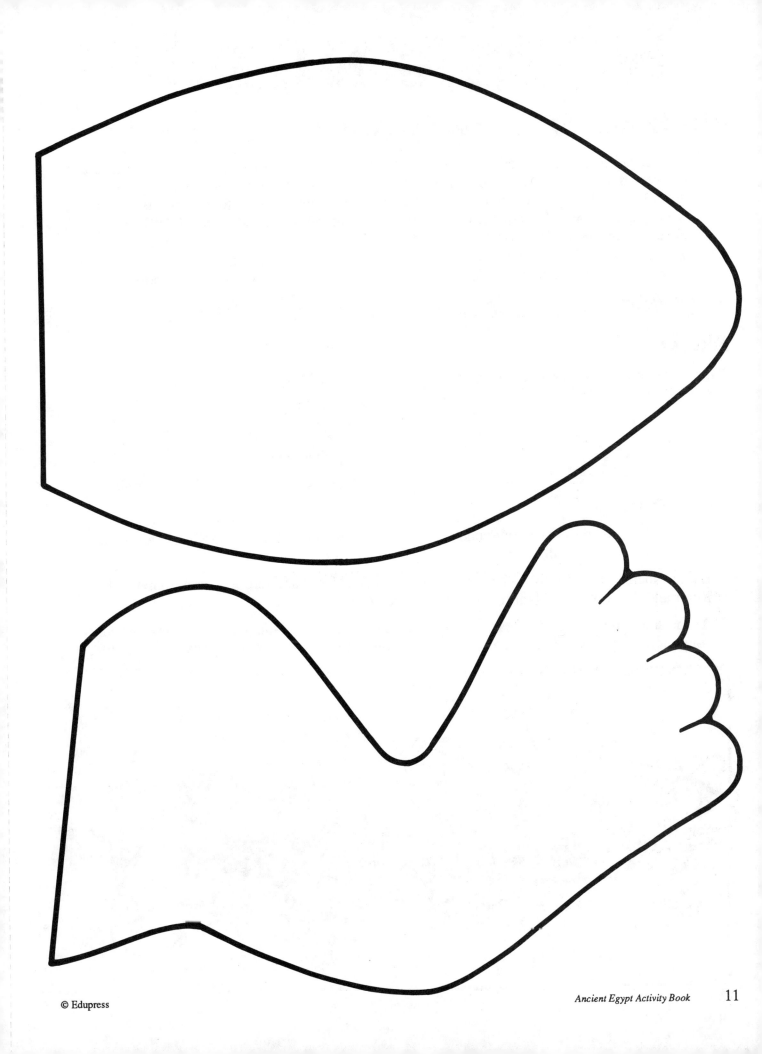

THE NILE

HISTORICAL AID

The ancient Egyptian civilization would never have existed without the Nile River. Egypt is a very dry land and it seldom rains. Without the yearly flooding of the Nile, Egypt would be a dry desert. Every year around July 15th, the river would begin to rise and by October it would spread over the land leaving a thick layer of black mud that the Egyptians used for growing their crops. This land was called the "black land". The Nile is the longest river in the world. It flows from south to north originating in the mountains of Central Africa. Besides farmland, the Nile also provided the Egyptians with water, fish, game and transportation.

PROJECT

Paint a cooperative mural of the Nile River.

MATERIALS

- Tempera paint
- Sponges
- Construction paper
- Butcher paper
- Glue

DIRECTIONS

1. Cut long lengths of butcher paper enough to stretch around the room, if possible. Tape or pin the butcher paper to the wall.

2. Have students look closely at the map of Egypt. Use sponges and tempera paint to make the Nile River and the shore and plant life surrounding the river.

3. As the students study different historical facts about life on the Nile, have them paint or cut out construction paper replicas of ancient boats, houses, temples, pyramids, shrines and wildlife.

PAPYRUS

HISTORICAL AID 🔲🔲🔲🔲🔲🔲🔲🔲🔲🔲🔲🔲🔲🔲🔲🔲🔲🔲🔲🔲🔲

Papyrus is a reed that grew in abundance in the shallow water of the Nile River. The Egyptians made baskets, boats, pens and paper from papyrus.

Paper was made from papyrus by peeling off the outer layers of the reed and chopping the remaining core into tiny pieces. The pieces were crossed and beaten together. The paper was smoothed with a polishing stone. Ink was made from soot and pens from sharpened reeds.

🔲🔲🔲🔲🔲🔲🔲🔲🔲🔲🔲🔲🔲🔲🔲🔲🔲🔲🔲🔲🔲🔲🔲🔲🔲🔲🔲🔲

PROJECT
Make paper for future hieroglyphic or writing activities.

DIRECTIONS

1. Tear or cut the newsprint into small pieces, 1/2 (1.27 cm) to 1-inch (2.54 cm) squares.

2. Soak the newsprint overnight in a large bowl with just enough water to cover it.

3. Add dryer lint and beat with an electric blender until the mixture is a puree.

4. Dissolve three tablespoons of cornstarch in two cups of water. Add to the puree.

5. When the pulp rises to the top of the bowl carefully slide a piece of window screen under the pulp. Lift the screen and drain the water.

6. Evenly spread the layer of pulp on the screen. Place the screen on several sheets of newspaper.

7. Cover with waxed paper and use bricks as weights to press water from the fibers. Allow the fibers to dry overnight.

8. Remove the bricks and waxed paper and carefully peel the sheets of paper off the screen.

MATERIALS

- Paper, newsprint is best
- Lint from a dryer filter
- Small squares of window screen
- Waxed paper
- Electric blender or hand beater
- Newspaper
- Cornstarch
- Several bricks or heavy weight

EGYPTIAN SCRIBES

HISTORICAL AID

Most Egyptian children never went to school. As soon as they were old enough to work, the boys went to work with their fathers and the girls learned how to run a home. Boys of royal or wealthy families were trained to work as scribes. They spent their days memorizing classic text and learning the characters of Egyptian hieroglyphics. These students practiced their writing by copying proverbs. Archeologists have found the copybooks that these boys practiced on.

PROJECT

Create a scribe's scroll and write Egyptian proverbs on it.

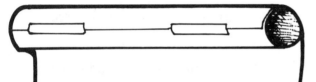

1. The glory of the King is in the sky, His power is in the horizon.

2. Food comes about by the hands, provisions by the feet.

3. You shall not spare your body when you are young.

4. Have regard for him who is shabbily dressed.

5. Do not accept the reward of the powerful.

MATERIALS

• Butcher paper

• Paper towel rolls—two per scroll

• Clear tape

• Yarn or string

DIRECTIONS

1. Cut butcher paper into 12-inch X 18-inch (18 cm X 27 cm) lengths.

2. Have students copy the Egyptian proverbs from the scroll at left or research and find your own.

3. Tape the top and the bottom of the butcher paper scroll to the paper towel rolls.

4. Roll up both sides toward the center and tie with yarn or string.

MEASUREMENT

HISTORICAL AID

The cubit was a measurement of length used by the ancient Egyptians. It was based on the length of the forearm from the tip of the middle finger to the elbow. The Royal cubit was actually about 21 inches or 53 centimeters.

The Ancient Egyptians also devised a method for measuring distances accurately by tying equally spaced knots in long ropes. This was important for measuring land each year after the Nile overflowed.

PROJECT

Work cooperatively to measure distances with cubits and ropes with equally spaced knots.

MATERIALS

- Six-foot lengths of string or rope
- Paper and pencils

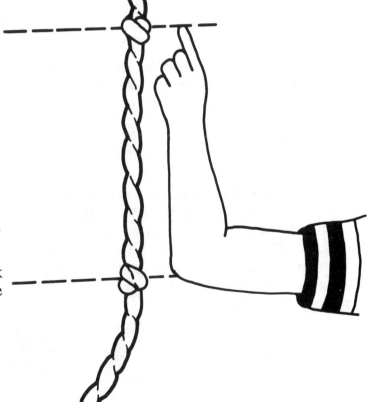

DIRECTIONS

1. Students can work with a partner.

2. Each pair should be given a 6 foot (2 meters) length of rope or string. Have each pair measure a cubit on their rope and tie a knot at that point. A cubit is the length of the forearm from the tip of the middle finger to the elbow. Continue to measure a cubit and tie a knot at that point. Make sure each knot on the rope is equally spaced.

3. When the amount of cubits on each rope or string has been determined, try measuring areas in the classroom or around the school.

4. For example, measure the cubits from your desk to the teacher's desk. Another example might be to measure the cubits around the classroom or the perimeter of a desk.

NUMBER BOW

HISTORICAL AID ▨▨▨▨▨▨▨▨▨▨▨▨▨▨▨▨▨▨▨▨▨▨▨▨

Egyptians used a pictorial representation for their numbers. See the symbol chart below. They wrote the pictures in ascending order, thus ones were written on the left, then tens, hundreds, thousands, etc. Five hundred twenty-one would be written by putting a one tally, two heel bones and five coils of rope. Example:

I∩∩ϱϱϱϱϱ

▨▨▨▨▨▨▨▨▨▨▨▨▨▨▨▨▨▨▨▨▨▨▨▨▨▨▨▨▨▨▨▨

PROJECT

Become familiar with numerical pictures by playing the Egyptian number bow game.

MATERIALS

- Reproduced copies of the number bow game board on the opposite page
- Colored ink pens
- Pair of dice

DIRECTIONS

1. This game is played with two players. Each needs a copy of the number bow game board.

2. Each player takes turns rolling the dice. Add the two dice together to find the total. Find the Egyptian symbol for the number. Color that part of the number bow.

3. The first one to completely color their number bow is the winner.

4. *Variation*—For a more challenging game, change the symbols on the number bow to represent larger numbers. Make number cards that can be drawn from a pile. The player draws a number, translates it to Egyptian symbols, matches it to a space on the number bow and colors in that space.

NAME OF SYMBOL

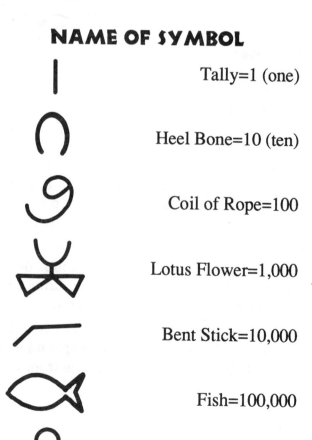

Tally=1 (one)

Heel Bone=10 (ten)

Coil of Rope=100

Lotus Flower=1,000

Bent Stick=10,000

Fish=100,000

Astonished Man=1,000,000

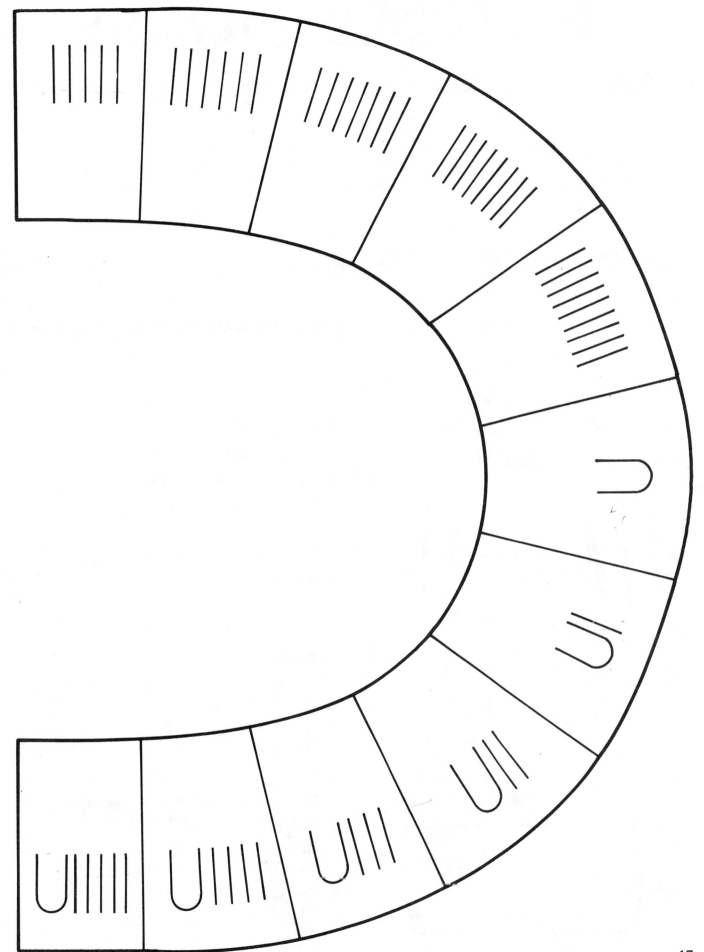

PADDLE DOLLS

HISTORICAL AID

The Egyptians made toys including balls, dolls and toy animals. They made their dolls out of wood, with hair made of clay beads attached with twine. Dolls may have been for children or they may have been made to put in someone's tomb to act as a companion in the afterlife.

PATTERN

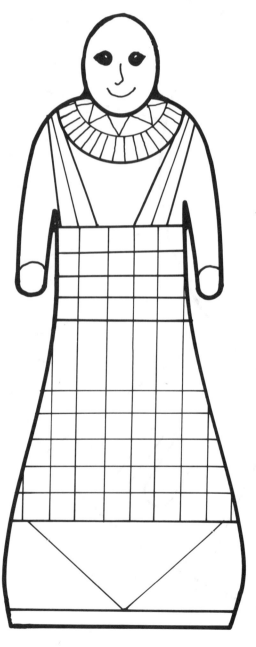

PROJECT

Make an Egyptian paddle doll.

MATERIALS

- Sturdy cardboard
- Yarn in dark colors of black or brown
- Bead macaroni dyed or painted brown or black
- Paint or colored ink pens
- Glue or staples
- Scissors

DIRECTIONS

1. Reproduce the paddle doll pattern and glue to the cardboard.

2. Cut out the pattern and cardboard at the same time.

3. Color or paint the doll's face and clothes.

4. Cut the yarn into 5" (13 cm) lengths. Cut eight pieces for each doll.

5. String three dyed or painted macaroni beads on each piece of yarn.

6. Glue or staple the yarn hair to the head of the paddle doll.

RECREATION

HISTORICAL AID

Through various artifacts, historians have shown that the Ancient Egyptians were fun-loving people who valued their recreational activities. Families loved to hunt and fish together. Girls played with dolls and boys wrestled and played soldier. The children played leapfrog and tip cat, a game played with a small oblong piece of wood called a "cat". The "cat" was struck into the air by a player who tried to hit it over a large ring in the ground. Balls were made of clay or plant fiber. Ball games were played while riding piggy-back or while leaping high into the air. Chariot racing was a favorite activity for the adults.

PROJECT

Plan and participate in an Egyptian game day.

DIRECTIONS

1. *Tip Cat* —Substitute a chalkboard eraser for a piece of wood. Draw a chalk circle with a 10 foot (3 meter) diameter. One child stands inside the circle. The other players stand on the perimeter. The player in the middle hits the eraser with the palm of the hand and sends it to the perimeter of the circle. A player at the perimeter tries to catch the eraser. The player who makes the catch takes the place in the center of the circle and the game continues.

2. *Leapfrog* —Two players take turns leaping over each other.

3. *Handball* —Players take turns hitting a ball against the wall.

4. *Chariot Races* —Students pair-up and have wheelbarrow races pretending they are chariots.

MATERIALS

- Chalkboard eraser
- Chalk
- Rubber playground balls

EGYPTIAN WIGS

HISTORICAL AID

Most Egyptians did not have long hair, in fact, many shaved their heads. Instead, they wore heavy, black wigs of sheep's wool or human hair, both for beauty and for protection from the hot climate.

Some of these wigs had three layers of curls on them. Beeswax was carefully applied to the wig to keep it neat looking. Headdresses, either embroidered or striped, were sometimes worn over the wig. Elaborate head ornaments and crowns were signs of the wearer's social position.

PROJECT

Fashion an Egyptian wig.

MATERIALS

- Large paper bags (grocery bags)
- Black tempera paint
- Tape
- Scissors
- White construction paper
- Colored pens, glitter, feathers and sequins
- Black yarn
- Glue

DIRECTIONS

1. Cut the paper bag in half, lengthwise, as shown.

2. Cut through the middle of the bag, horizontally. Overlap the halves of the bag to size on head.

3. When the correct size is found, tape the halves together.

4. Paint the bag black.

5. Glue lengths of black yarn in layers and curls to cover the black bag.

6. Cut a length of white construction paper to fit around the wig. Staple or tape ends together.

7. Decorate the head ornament using colored pens, glitter feathers and sequins.

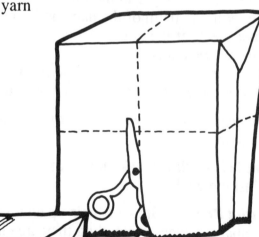

MAKEUP

HISTORICAL AID

Men and women painted their eyes with powdered grey galenea or kohl and a green copper oxide called *malachite*. Some fat would be mixed with the makeup when it was applied to the face. A green line was applied above the eye and a grey line below. This made the eyes look larger and also protected them from disease. The women also colored their lips and cheeks with red ochre and their hands with henna. Ornate mirrors, applicators and combs have been found to house these cosmetics. The women wore cones of scented ointment on their heads. As the evening wore on, the cones would melt and their perfume would fill the air.

PROJECT

Work in pairs to apply Egyptian makeup.

MATERIALS

- Gray and green eyeshadow
- Red lipstick

DIRECTIONS

1. Apply gray eyeshadow to the top lid of the eye and green eyeshadow to the lower part of the eye.

2. Color lips and cheeks with the red lipstick.

3. Don your wigs (see page 20) to complete the effect.

EGYPTIAN COLLARS

HISTORICAL AID

The Egyptians were lovers of beauty and fashion. Wealthy Egyptian men and women adorned themselves with beautiful jewelry. Since all gold belonged to the pharaoh, any gold jewelry would have either been a gift from the pharaoh or made out of gold stolen from tombs. Ordinary people adorned themselves with bracelets, earrings, necklace collars and anklets made of semi-precious beads such as lapis-lazuli and turqoise.

PROJECT

Make an Egyptian collar necklace.

Two different projects are suggested.

MATERIALS

- Drinking straws—six per necklace
- Needles
- Floss or heavy thread
- Scissors
- White construction paper

DIRECTIONS

1. Cut floss or thread long enough to fit comfortably around the neck.

2. Cut the straws in half.

3. Use the needle and thread to sew the straws together approximately one-half inch (1.25 cm) from the top. Leave enough floss at each end to tie around the neck.

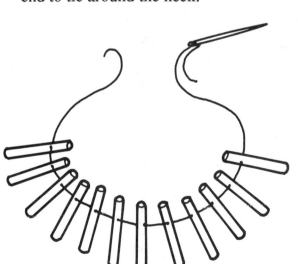

1. Color half of a sheet of construction paper in brilliant colors and interesting designs.

2. Cut as shown below.

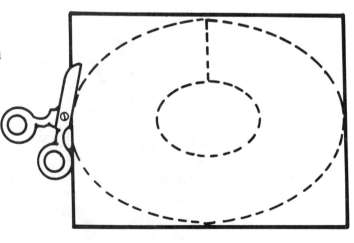

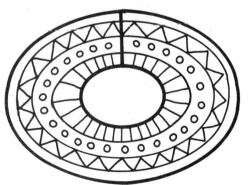

CLOTHING

HISTORICAL AID 𝄢𝄢𝄢𝄢𝄢𝄢𝄢𝄢𝄢𝄢𝄢𝄢𝄢𝄢𝄢𝄢𝄢𝄢𝄢𝄢𝄢

In Egypt's hot weather, people needed light, loose-fitting and easily washed clothes. Linen, which was a fabric made from plant fiber, was the perfect cloth. The Egyptian women usually wore tunics. These were made by folding a rectangle of cloth in half, sewing it on the sides, leaving room for the arms and cutting a keyhole for the neck. Sleeves and elaborate pleats were often added to the tunics.

The men usually wore short kilts or loincloths made out of fine linen. Cloaks were gradually developed for use as overgarments.

PROJECT

Make Egyptian tunics and kilts.

MATERIALS

- Fabric or butcher paper
- White towels
- Scissors
- Needle and thread or masking tape

DIRECTIONS

1. To make a tunic, fold a length of fabric or butcher paper in half.

2. Sew or glue the open sides together, leaving room on each side for an armhole.

3. Cut a half circle out of the top fold for the neckline.

4. To make the kilt use a white towel and wrap around the waist leaving an end of the towel to tuck inside to keep it secure.

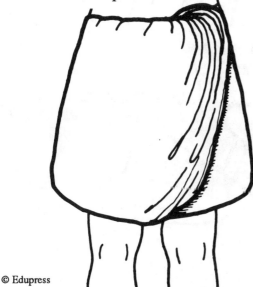

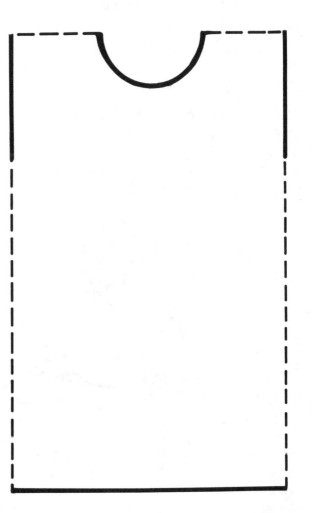

VILLAGE CRAFTS

HISTORICAL AID

Village craftsmen usually included a coppersmith, a potter, a jeweler, a charm and amulet maker, a carpenter, a paper maker and a cloth weaver. Coppersmiths made tools, weapons and jars by hammering copper or by casting molten copper in clay molds. Carpenters and goldsmiths made coffins, amulets and funeral goods as well as furniture and jewelry for the wealthy. Weaving of cloth was usually done by women in a workshop with a horizontal loom. The finishing of the cloth was done by a craftsman who specialized in this field. Potters used wheels which were turned by hand to shape pots. The craftsmen would usually barter their handiwork at the village market.

PROJECT

Make a variety of crafts to barter in a cooperative activity at a village market.

DIRECTIONS

1. Divide into four cooperative groups.

2. Tell each group that they represent an Egyptian artisan in the village community.

3. Ask them to create a craft appropriate to their trade. They may use the suggestions that follow or create original crafts.

4. When crafts are complete, allow children to barter with each other and exchange for a new craft.

MATERIALS

- Cardboard or construction paper
- Styrofoam meat trays
- Clay
- Aluminum foil
- Sequins
- Glue
- Gold spray paint
- Bowl
- Scissors
- Flat white sheet
- Markers or crayons
- Tempera paint
- Staples
- Paint brushes

COPPERSMITH

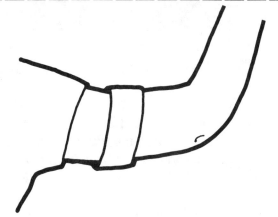

PROJECT
Make bracelets or headbands out of aluminum foil and spray paint with gold.

DIRECTIONS
1. Cut cardboard or construction paper to fit upper arm for an armband or to fit around head for a headband.
2. Cover with aluminum foil and spray paint gold.
3. Staple or glue ends together.

JEWELER

PROJECT
Make amulets and charms.

DIRECTIONS
1. Cut patterns for amulets and charms out of styrofoam meat trays and spray gold.
2. Glue sequins to simulate the semiprecious stones that jewelers used in ancient Egypt.

POTTER

PROJECT
Make a clay bowl.

DIRECTIONS
1. Shape a clay pot by using an aluminum bowl as a mold.
2. Allow to dry and either fire in a kiln or keep as greenware.
3. Paint and decorate with hieroglyphics or Egyptian figures or glaze and refire.

CLOTHMAKER

PROJECT
Design your own Egyptian cloth.

DIRECTIONS
1. Cut a flat white sheet into equal-sized squares.
2. Use fabric markers to decorate a square with original shapes or designs.
3. Add sequins and mount on cardboard, if desired.

MARKET PLACE

HISTORICAL AID

At the village market in ancient Egypt, people cooked and shopped outdoors because of the warm climate. Shopping was done by bartering because there was no currency or money. Sellers established the value of their goods in *deben*, a fixed weight of gold, silver or copper. The buyer had to offer something worth as many deben in exchange. A goat was valued at one deben and a bed was worth 2.5 deben. The Egyptians bartered their copper, grain, linen, papyrus and semi-precious stones for wood, gold, ostrich feathers and ivory. Farmers bartered their crops for magical charms, metal knives and pots.

PROJECT

Students will plan and hold an open market with bartering as a means of purchasing goods.

Follow-up with discussion about cost comparison, equal values and greater-than, less-than concepts.

MATERIALS

• Towels

• Small items for bartering

DIRECTIONS

1. Each participating student should bring a towel and several small objects from home that they are willing to trade.

2. Designate a deben as a basis for determining value. Students should figure out and mark how many debens their articles are worth.

3. On market day, each student needs to find an area to lay out their towel and arrange their bartering objects.

4. Open up the market for business and let the students barter for other objects. This can be done in small groups or as a whole class.

GARDEN

HISTORICAL AID 📜📜📜📜📜📜📜📜📜📜📜📜📜📜📜📜

The yearly flood of the Nile gave Egypt its rich farming land. The lands were flooded during the summer, but by October the ground was covered by a rich dark layer of silt that was ready for the farmers to plow and sow. Egyptian farmers grew vegetables such as onions, garlic, leeks, beans, lentils and lettuce. They grew barley and wheat which were the main staples of their diet. They also grew gourds, dates, figs, cucumbers, melons and grapes. However, they grew no citrus fruit trees because the weather was too hot for these types of trees to survive.

PROJECT

Plan and participate in planting an Egyptian garden.

MATERIALS

- Small planting containers or an outdoor garden plot
- Rich top soil
- Barley, wheat, onion, garlic, leek, bean, lentil, lettuce, cucumber and melon seeds
- A source of water—hose or watering can
- Small sticks
- A hoe
- Staples

DIRECTIONS

1. Prepare the soil by mixing up the top soil.

2. Plant seeds according to package directions.

3. Label plants by stapling the seed package on a small stick and placing in the ground by the area where those seeds are planted.

4. Water as directed.

5. Watch your Egyptian garden grow.

6. When plants are ready to harvest, plan an Egyptian feast.

ESTATE

HISTORICAL AID

The ancient Egyptians built their villages and towns along the banks of the Nile or crowded around government buildings. Most Egyptian homes were built of dried mud-bricks. Wealthy families often built country estates on the outskirts of the towns. The estates were built around a large, central reception hall with bedrooms and private apartments surrounding it. They also included servant's quarters and lush gardens. Grille windows, built high on the walls, let in little sunlight, caught the breeze and kept the rooms cool.

PROJECT

Make a cooperative diorama depicting four different aspects of life on an Egyptian estate.

DIRECTIONS

1. Divide students into groups of four. Each student in the group chooses a different part of the estate from the following pages to depict in a diorama. Materials and directions are given for each suggestion.

2. Each group cuts one 18" (46 cm) diameter circle out of the tagboard square. Divide and cut the circle into four equal pieces, one for each student in the group.

3. Give each student a large sheet of construction paper. Paint or color a background scene that corresponds with the part of the estate they have chosen to depict. Make a 1-inch (2.54 cm) fold along the length of the painted background. When dry, fold the paper in half across the width.

4. Glue the 1-inch (2.54 cm) fold to the straight sides of the quarter circle, as shown. Add foreground props and details.

5. When the individual dioramas are completed, staple or tape the four parts together to complete the circle.

MATERIALS

- 12" by 18" (30 cm X 46 cm) construction paper
- 18" (46 cm) squares of tagboard
- Glue
- Staples or tape
- Paint or crayons

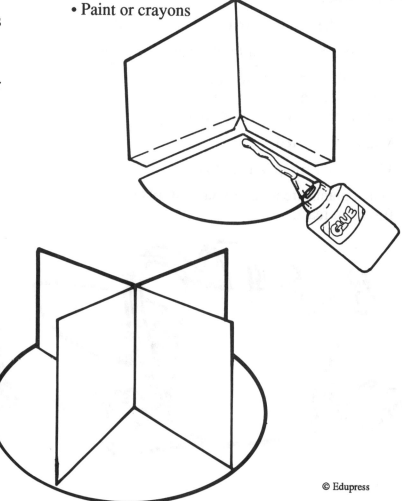

FARMLAND

Peasant farmers worked the owner's land around his estate and in return gave back some of the food and livestock they raised. A steward had an area on the estate where the farmers could bring their livestock and grain to be counted.

MATERIALS

- Colored tissue paper
- Construction paper
- Various pens and paint
- Plastic farm animals
- Glue
- Scissors

DIRECTIONS

1. Cut a construction paper mat for the steward to sit on.

2. Make tissue paper vegetables. Draw, color and cut out the steward and his scribe. Glue in position on the mat.

3. Surround the steward and his scribe with piles of vegetables and livestock cut-outs. Use plastic farm animals, if desired.

GRAINERY SILOS

The grain the farmers delivered was stored on the estate in silos made of dried mud shaped like a bee hive. The silos had openings at the top to put the grain in and on the side to take the grain out. The grain was ground into flour and used to make bread.

MATERIALS

- White egg-shaped pantyhose containers
- Brown construction paper
- Various colored ink pens
- Black permanent marker

DIRECTIONS

1. Take the larger side of the pantyhose container and glue the open side to the base of the diorama.

2. Use the black permanent marker to draw a "hole" at the top and a small door on the side.

3. Cut out a brown construction paper ladder to go from the base of the silo to the top.

4. Draw and cut out pictures of servants grinding the grain and place by the silos.

STABLES

An Egyptian estate usually included a stable. The stable was filled with horses and chariots. These were used for hunting in the desert. Horse-drawn chariots were introduced to the Egyptians around 1700 B.C. by the Hyskos and were also used in battle.

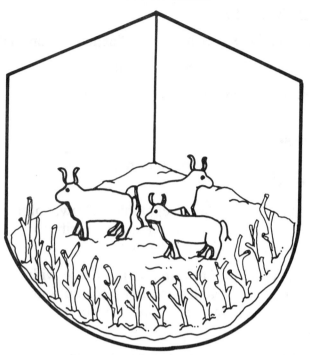

MATERIALS

- Popsicle sticks or twigs
- Plastic horse figures or magazine pictures of horses
- Clay or styrofoam

DIRECTIONS

1. Build a fence enclosure by sticking twigs into a clay or styrofoam base.

2. Bring miniature plastic horses or cut pictures from magazines, mount on cardboard and display inside enclosure.

LOTUS POOL

An Egyptian's estate usually had a lotus pool as its central feature. This shallow pool served as a decoration, but was also stocked with lotus plants and ornamental fish. The water in the pool was replaced regularly by the servants to keep it fresh. Poolside borders were planted with decorative plants and trees such as sycamore figs, date palms and acacia. The lotus plant, or Egyptian water lily, grew on a very weak stalk and spread out upon the surface of the water. This plant has white or purple flowers that may be one foot across.

MATERIALS

- Green, blue, white and purple construction paper
- Small rocks or pebbles (optional)
- Crayons   • Glue

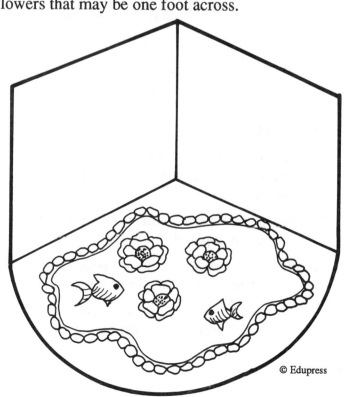

DIRECTIONS

1. Cut blue construction paper for the lotus pool and glue it to the base of the diorama. Decorate the pool's edge with a colorful pattern or small stones.

2. Make lotus blossoms to "float" in the pool by gluing white or purple paper petals to a green circular base.

3. Color, cut and glue fish to the pool.

BEDROOM

Bedrooms were furnished with beds made of wooden frames with leather straps and a wooden headrest that kept the bugs off their faces. The bathrooms had a wooden seat with a pot of sand beneath, which the servants emptied. The floors were covered with woven mats and the walls were brightly painted.

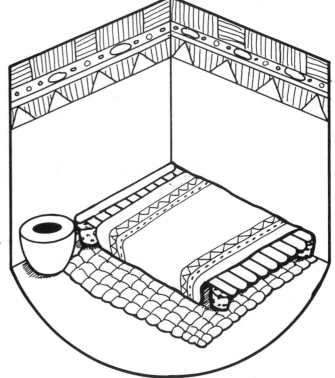

MATERIALS

- Small half of egg-shaped pantyhose container
- Black permanent marker
- Sand
- Popsicle sticks
- Glue
- Paint
- Small piece of cloth
- Bottle corks

DIRECTIONS

1. Design a woven mat for the floor.

2. Glue popsicle sticks together to construct a bed. Use bottle corks cut in half for a base. Drape cloth for a blanket.

3. Glue small half of pantyhose container with the open end up. Fill with sand. Cover with cardboard with a hole cut in the center.

RECEPTION HALL

The reception hall was located in the front of the house with all the other rooms around it. It was a large pillared room where important guests were entertained. It had very few furniture pieces other than a few chairs and a table. The walls were brightly painted with beautiful designs. This is the room Egyptians would use to host parties and feasts.

MATERIALS

- Construction paper
- Colored ink pens
- Tape
- Glue
- Popsicle sticks

DIRECTIONS

1. Decorate construction paper with designs. Cut, roll and tape into several columns to glue to the base.

2. Design borders with construction paper to put on the background walls.

3. Construct tables and chairs with popsicle sticks and glue in place on the diorama. Small doll furniture may also be used.

4. Include Egyptian people, if desired.

FEAST

HISTORICAL AID

Ancient Egyptians did not enjoy a wide variety of foods. However, they usually had an abundance of healthy things to eat because of the ease with which crops grew in the fertile valleys. Some favorite foods included figs, dates and honey. Bread was the main staple of their diet. They also grew beans, cabbages, cucumbers, lettuce, peas, radishes and fruits such as melons and grapes. They harvested fish from the Nile and hunted ducks. Egyptian families raised cattle, geese, goats and sheep.

PROJECT

Plan and prepare a feast in which students sample a variety of foods eaten by the people of ancient Egypt.

MATERIALS

- Towels or pillows for each student to sit on
- Plates
- Trays
- Bowls of water
- Student-supplied food from the following list:

bread	cucumbers
figs	lettuce
dates	peas
honey	beans
raisins	cabbage
grapes	melon
radishes	

DIRECTIONS

1. Ask each student to bring a food item from the list to share with other students. Food should be prepared and put on trays to be passed.

2. Seat students on towels in a circle on the floor.

3. Supply each student with a bowl of water.

4. Students can take turns passing food to each other and trying the simple foods from the trays. Be sure they wash their hands prior to sampling.

5. Students may choose to dress for the feast in the clothing and jewelry they have made in the other projects.

EGYPTIAN BREAD

HISTORICAL AID

Ancient papyri records show the Egyptians made over thirty types of bread, the main staple of their diet. The yearly flooding of the Nile Valley enabled the regular cultivation of wheat in abundant supplies for bread-making.

The Egyptians developed the technology of natural yeast and its use in leavened bread. They found that a mixture of wheat, flour and water left to sit in a warm place for a few days would ferment and develop the yeast that causes bread to rise.

PROJECT

Observe the leavening process by baking an Egyptian sourdough fig roll.

DIRECTIONS

1. Combine 2 cups white flour and 2 cups water in a glass bowl and allow to stand uncovered for 3 days in a warm place, stirring occasionally. This is called the *starter*. Add 2 cups wheat flour and 2 cups warm water to the starter. Blend well. Cover and let sit for 8 to 10 hours or overnight in a warm spot. This mixture is called *sponge*.

2. Combine 2 cups sponge and 2 cups warm water. Add 2 cups wheat flour, salt, honey, cinnamon and oil. Knead the dough for 10 minutes to a smooth, dry texture on a floured board. Add small amounts of flour or water if necessary.

3. Use a floured rolling pin to roll the dough into a square or rectangle about 1/2-inch (1.27 cm) thick. Spread the fig preserves over the rolled dough and sprinkle on the sesame seeds. Roll up into a cylinder. Slit the top with a knife, place in a greased baking pan, and let sit for 1 to 3 hours, depending on the warmth of the kitchen. Brush tops with water during the rising and baking. Bake in a preheated oven at 350 degrees for one hour.

MATERIALS

- 2 cups (473.2 ml) white flour
- Water
- 4 cups (946.4 ml) whole wheat flour
- 1 teaspoon (4.9 ml) salt
- 3 tablespoons (44.4 ml) honey
- 1 teaspoon (4.9 ml) cinnamon
- 1 cup (236.6 ml) fig preserves
- 1/4 cup (59.15 ml) sesame seeds
- Small glass bowl
- Medium bowl
- Breadboard

KING TUT MASK

HISTORICAL AID

By 1600 B.C. robbers had ransacked many of the pyramids. Later pharaohs decided that their bodies would be safer in hidden tombs cut from solid rock. Many of these pharaohs chose to have their tombs built in the isolated cliffs of the Valley of the Kings.

Pharaoh Tutankhamun, King Tut, was buried here. The young king died when he was only 19 years old. His tomb contained jewelry, weapons, furniture, musical instruments and many artifacts made of precious stones and gold. One of the most famous and beautiful articles found was the magnificent gold death mask which was placed on Tutankhamun's mummy.

PROJECT

Create a replica of King Tut's death mask.

MATERIALS

- Cardboard or poster board
- Glue
- Blue and yellow tempera paint
- Brushes

DIRECTIONS

1. Reproduce and cut out the pattern at right.

2. Trace the pattern on cardboard and cut along the traced outline.

3. Glue the pattern to the cardboard.

4. Use the blue and yellow tempera to paint stripes on the mask. Paint the face yellow. When dry, outline the eyes with blue paint.

5. Use the mask to decorate the room or use as a book cover for stories about King Tutankhamun.

CROOK

HISTORICAL AID

The Egyptians believed the pharaoh was a living god. Re, the sun god, was the first mythical king of Egypt and every pharaoh was his son. Everything and everyone belonged to the pharaoh. He had total control over the Egyptian people because he represented the wishes of the gods.

The pharaoh wore certain objects to signify his authority. The crook, resembling a small cane, symbolized the pharaoh's position as king and shepherd of his people.

PROJECT

Make an Egyptian pharaoh's crook.

MATERIALS

- Thin cardboard wrapping paper tubes or rolled poster board
- Aluminum foil
- Clear tape
- Tempera paint
- Paint brush

DIRECTIONS

1. Roll a 12-inch (30 cm) length of aluminum foil around the end of the paper tube.
2. Tape the aluminum foil to the end of the tube.
3. Shape and pinch aluminum foil into a hook.
4. Paint the remainder of the paper tube.

FLAIL

HISTORICAL AID

The flail was a tool with a heavy, wooden club hinged to swing freely from a long handle and was used to thresh grain. The flail often appeared in paintings of the pharaohs and symbolized the fertility of the land. The pharaohs and many of the Egyptian gods carried the crook and flail together and crossed them over the chest as a symbol of their position as leader and protector of the Egyptian people.

PROJECT

Make an Egyptian pharaoh's flail.

MATERIALS

- Full sheet of construction paper
- Masking tape
- Yarn—variety of colors
- Colored beads and buttons (optional)

DIRECTIONS

1. Roll sheet of construction paper into a tube and tape together.
2. Fold four inches (12 cm) from top.
3. Tape yarn streamers to opening.
4. Tie beads or buttons to yarn (optional).

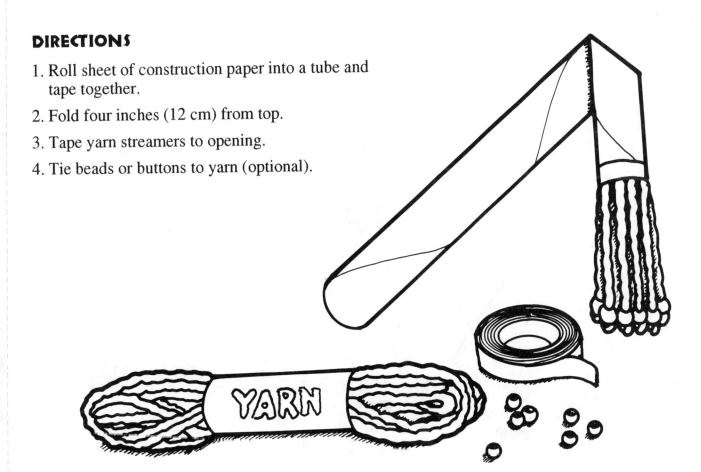

PYRAMIDS

HISTORICAL AID

The great pyramids of Egypt are the oldest stone buildings in the world. These ancient structures were built as tombs for their kings. The kings, who were called *pharaohs*, had pyramids built to preserve their bodies for their life after death. They were built to house not only the pharaoh's body but all his treasures and the goods he would need in his next life. These ancient tombs were gigantic; the largest is as big as a 40-story building and covers the area of ten football fields. Thousands of men were needed to build these huge structures. It took up to 20 years to build one pyramid.

PROJECT

Construct a folded paper pyramid using the pattern on the facing page.

MATERIALS

- Construction paper: white, light brown or tan.
- Scissors
- Tape
- Pens or pencils

DIRECTIONS

1. Make copies of the pyramid pattern on the facing page.
2. Cut on dotted lines.
3. Fold on thick lines.
4. Tape together into a pyramid.

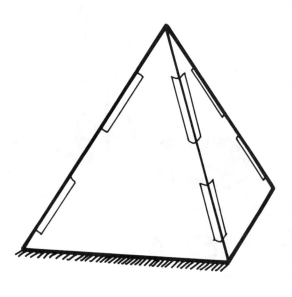

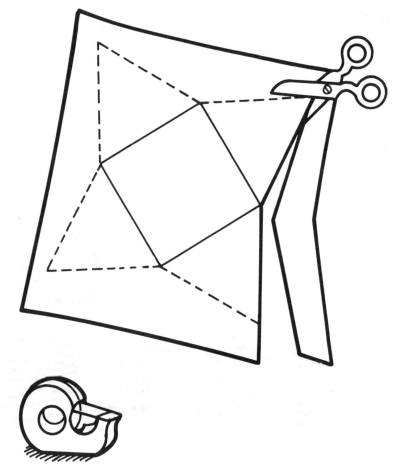

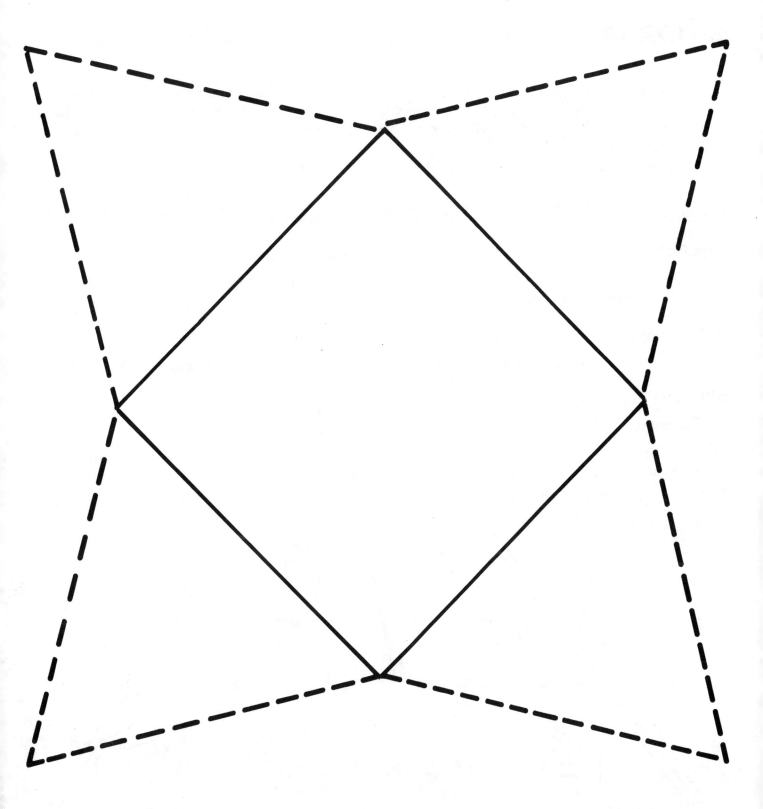

PYRAMID TOMBS

HISTORICAL AID

The main purpose of the pyramid tombs was to safeguard the pharaoh's body. Fake burial chambers, secret passageways and granite doors were constructed in order to safeguard the pharaoh's body and possessions. The pyramid tomb was only part of the funeral site. There was a mortuary temple attached to the front of the pyramid tomb and a long causeway which linked it to the Nile. Small pyramid tombs were built nearby for the pharaoh's wives.

PROJECT

Cooperative group project—design your own interior for a modern-day pyramid.

MATERIALS

- Large sheets of butcher paper
- Pens, pencils, paints and brushes

DIRECTIONS

1. Divide into cooperative groups of three or four students. Give each group a large piece of butcher paper.

2. Have students brainstorm unique and different ideas to include in a modern pyramid such as swimming pools, color TV or basketball courts.

3. When students have finished the brainstorming process, ask them to draw the floor plan and furnishings for the interior design of their pyramid. Remind them to include ancient features such as fake chambers and secret passageways. Have each group take classmates on a "guided tour" of their pyramid.

TEMPLE OF AMON-RE

HISTORICAL AID 🔲🔲🔲🔲🔲🔲🔲🔲🔲🔲🔲🔲🔲🔲🔲🔲🔲🔲🔲🔲🔲🔲🔲🔲🔲

Amon-Re was the most important god in ancient Egyptian mythology and was known as the King of the Gods. A huge temple was built in his honor in the city of Karnac. The Great Hall of the temple, completed by King Ramses II in the 1200's B.C., was the largest columned hall ever built. The 78-foot (24-meter) columns were adorned with brilliantly colored relief paintings of Egyptian people, animals and various hieroglyphics.

🔲🔲🔲🔲🔲🔲🔲🔲🔲🔲🔲🔲🔲🔲🔲🔲🔲🔲🔲🔲🔲🔲🔲🔲🔲🔲🔲🔲🔲🔲🔲🔲

PROJECT

Work cooperatively to make a relief painted column to duplicate the same height as the columns found in the Great Hall of the Temple of Amon-Re.

MATERIALS

- Butcher paper
- Colored ink pens or paint
- Tape
- Hieroglyphic patterns for copying

DIRECTIONS

1. Each of 26 students will need a piece of butcher paper three feet long.

2. Paint or color each column section with hieroglyphics, Egyptian symbols, animals or people. When painting characters, refer to Egyptian Painting Style (page 7) to follow the strict rules ancient artists had for painting characters.

3. Roll and tape the paper to create a column three feet tall.

4. Go outside and ask students to place their column sections end to end to measure 78 feet. This will duplicate the actual column height. Ask them to imagine long rows of these huge, colorful columns.

5. Individual columns can be displayed in the classroom for viewing.

MUMMIES

HISTORICAL AID 🏛️🏛️🏛️🏛️🏛️🏛️🏛️🏛️🏛️🏛️🏛️🏛️🏛️🏛️🏛️🏛️🏛️🏛️

The ancient Egyptians believed in life after death and made elaborate preparations for death and burial. They spent centuries developing a process known as *mummification,* which prevented the body from decaying and preserved it for its role in the afterlife.

This process could take as long as 70 days. First, the vital organs were taken out of the corpse and put into jars. The body was dried for 40 days, then treated with a molten resin and wrapped in many layers of linen material. The bound head was covered with a portrait mask and the entire mummy was wrapped in one more linen layer and coated with resin.

PROJECT

Learn how the Egyptians mummified people by mummifying a balloon.

MATERIALS

• Long balloons

• Scissors

• Wallpaper paste

• Newspaper cut into strips

• Small bowl

• Black tempera paint

• Paint brush

DIRECTIONS

1. Blow up a long balloon and tie the end of it.

2. Cut or tear strips of newspaper.

3. Put wallpaper paste into a small, shallow bowl and dip the strips of newspaper into it. Cover each piece with the paste.

4. Wrap each strip around the balloon until you have completely covered the balloon with one layer. Allow it to dry.

5. Apply another layer for sturdiness, if desired, and allow it to dry completely.

6. Using black tempera paint, outline the mummy's arms and face.

SARCOPHAGUS

HISTORICAL AID

The completed mummy was placed inside a single coffin or nest of coffins. Some of these coffins were shaped like small houses, ovals or oblongs. Many were covered inside and out with elaborate inscriptions, hieroglyphics and figures of gods intended to protect the body from decay. Some coffins were made of gold and inlaid with lapis lazuli and other semi-precious stones.

The coffin was placed inside a large stone box, called a *sarcophagus*. Once placed inside the sarcophagus, the mummy was ready for its procession to its final resting place.

PROJECT

Make a coffin for a pop-up mummy to place inside a sarcophagus.

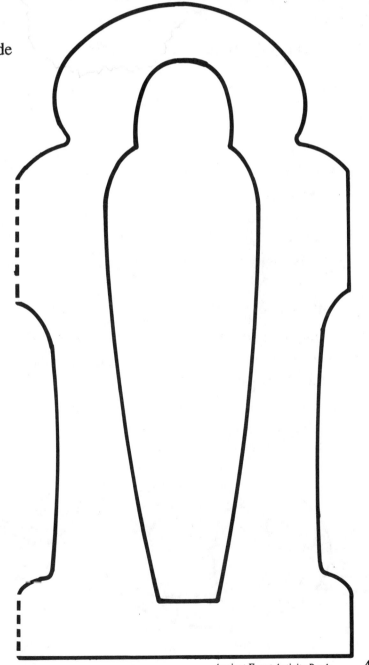

MATERIALS

- White construction paper
- Scissors
- Crayons or markers
- Staples

DIRECTIONS

1. Trace the larger pattern of the coffin at right onto white construction paper and cut out.

2. Trace and cut out the smaller pattern of the mummy onto white construction paper and cut out.

3. Fold the mummy in half and cut slits along the folded edge 1/2-inch (1.27 cm) apart to within 1/2-inch of the edge.

4. Unfold and staple inside the coffin.

5. Decorate around the mummy with hieroglyphics.

6. Optional—Place mummy and coffin in a small, decorated gift box or shoe box as the "sarcophagus".

SCARAB

HISTORICAL AID

The ancient Egyptians chose the scarab as a sacred symbol because of its process of laying its eggs in decaying matter where the young beetles hatch. This was a sign of rebirth to the Egyptians. Just as the scarab beetles were "reborn" from decay, the Egyptians, too, looked forward to rebirth after death.

The Egyptians made charms and jewelry in the shape of the scarab. Scarabs carved in precious stones are still used in jewelry and as good-luck charms.

PROJECT

Make a scarab paperweight out of bread dough.

MATERIALS

- 2 cups (473.2 ml) flour
- 1 cup (236.6 ml) salt
- 1 cup water
- Large bowl
- Baking sheet
- Toothpicks or popsicle sticks
- Tempera paint
- Felt
- Paint brushes
- Glue

DIRECTIONS

1. Mix the flour and salt together in a large mixing bowl. Slowly add the water while mixing until all the dry ingredients are moistened.

2. Remove mixture from the bowl and place onto a well-floured surface. Knead for about six to ten minutes.

3. Tear off a ball of dough about the size of your palm and shape it into an oval with a flat bottom.

4. Use a toothpick or a popsicle stick to carve the scarab as shown in the diagram.

5. Place scarab on a baking sheet and bake the in the oven at 325 degrees for 30 to 40 minutes or until golden brown.

6. When cool, paint the dough shape one color. Paint the carved beetle pattern a different color.

7. Glue a piece of felt to the bottom to prevent scratching and use as a paperweight.

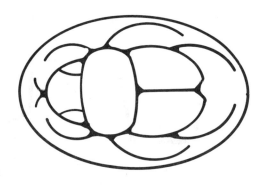 

THE GREAT SPHINX

HISTORICAL AID

The Egyptian sphinx, a mythical creature, had a head of a man and the body, legs, feet and tail of a lion. The lion's body represented the connection between the sun god and the pharaoh's role as the son of Re. Egyptian sculptors made the face resemble the current Pharaoh.

The Great Sphinx stands in the desert at Giza near the Great Pyramid in Egypt. It is thought to have been built 4,500 years ago for the pharaoh Kafre to guard the way to his pyramid. It is 240 feet (73 meters) long and 66 feet (20 meters) high. Its head and body are carved from solid rock and the paws and legs are built of stone blocks.

PROJECT

Create a mythical creature—part human, part animal.

DIRECTIONS

1. Cut a sheet of construction paper in half.

2. On one half of the paper, draw an animal body. This can be any animal.

3. On the second half of the paper, draw a self-portrait, face only.

4. Exchange the animal body with another student's animal body.

5. Assemble the new creature by taping animal body and self-portrait together.

6. Write a description of this newly-created mythical creature.

MATERIALS

• Full sheet of white construction paper

• Crayons

• Glue

• Scissors

CROWNS

HISTORICAL AID

Until 3100 B.C. Egypt was divided into two states: Upper Egypt and Lower Egypt. Upper Egypt included the territory south of the Delta on the two banks of the Nile. Lower Egypt occupied the Delta region. A king named Menes conquered Lower Egypt and formed a united kingdom with the capital located at Memphis.

Both Lower Egypt and Upper Egypt had separate crowns for their kings so Menes combined these two crowns for his united kingdom. This combined crown was worn by a pharaoh to signify his rule over all of Egypt. The white crown was originally the crown of Upper Egypt and the red crown was the crown of Lower Egypt.

PROJECT

Make two crowns of Egypt and combine them to signify rule over both Upper and Lower Egypt.

MATERIALS

- White construction paper 12" X 18" (30 cm X 46 cm)
- Red construction paper
- Blue or gold construction paper
- Stapler or tape
- Scissors
- Patterns

DIRECTIONS

1. Fold the white paper in half across the width.

2. Copy pattern for the white crown and cut out. Place the dotted line on the fold of the white paper. Trace around pattern and cut out.

3. Fit to head using extra strips of construction paper and secure with tape or staples.

4. Repeat steps 1-3 using the pattern for the red crown. Fit the red crown over the white crown using extra strips of red construction paper.

5. Put crown on head and mark a box where the the ear is. Cut out a hole large enough to fit around the ear. Cut a window for the forehead.

6. Using the illustration at right as a guide, draw and cut out a cobra from blue or gold construction paper. Bend back the cobra's tail and attach it to the front of the crown. Tape the head of the cobra to the crown so that it does not fall forward.

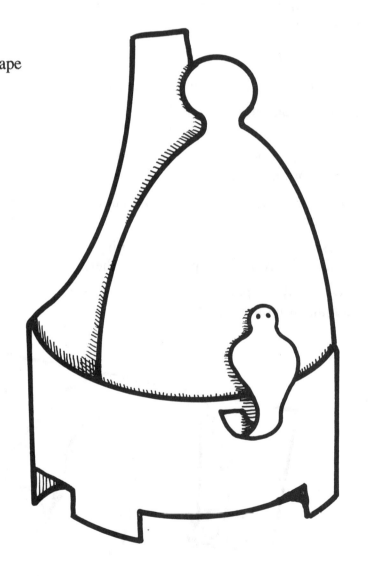

RED CROWN

Place dotted lines on fold

WHITE CROWN

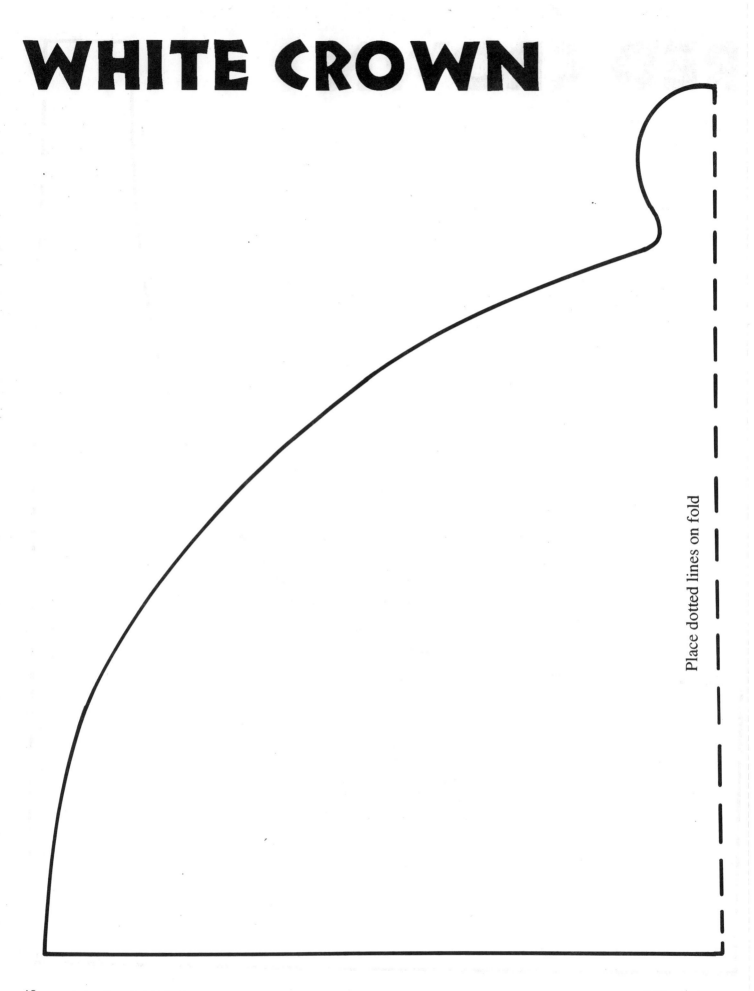

Place dotted lines on fold

Ancient Egypt Activity Book

© Edupress